326
I
c./

INGRAHAM, LEONARD
W

SLAVERY IN THE
UNITED STATES

© THE BAKER & TAYLOR CO.

SLAVERY IN THE UNITED STATES

A gang of slaves is moved to a market in the South.

SLAVERY IN THE UNITED STATES

By Leonard W. Ingraham

Illustrated with
photographs and drawings

FRANKLIN WATTS, INC.
845 Third Avenue, New York, N.Y. 10022

TO CLAIRE —
my devoted helpmate.

Photos courtesy of:

Library of Congress, pages 65, 69, 74, 77, 79

New York Historical Society, opp. title page, pages 6, 16, 22, 27, 32, 45, 75, 81

New York Public Library, Picture Collection, pages 4, 11, 14, 23, 24, 28, 31, 38, 41, 49, 54, 55, 59, 66, 67, 76

New York Public Library, Schomburg Collection, opp. page 1, pages 5, 8, 10, 15, 17, 26, 36, 40, 42, 43, 47, 48, 56, 57, 60, 61, 62, 63, 71, 73, 80

Old Print Shop, Inc., New York, page 35

SBN 531–00630–1

12   11   10   9   8

Library of Congress Catalog Card Number: 68-27402

Copyright © 1968 by Franklin Watts, Inc.

Printed in the United States of America

CONTENTS

Bidding at a slave auction in the southern United States.

INTRODUCTION

Abraham Lincoln, sixteenth President of the United States of America, sat thoughtfully at his big mahogany desk. It was spring and the great lawns of the White House were deepening from pale jade to vibrant green.

The year was 1865. The War Between the States was still going on and this was foremost in the heart and mind of President Lincoln. But, in his hand was a document containing the proposed Thirteenth Amendment to the Constitution of the United States — the abolition of slavery. Lincoln felt that the amendment had to be passed, and it was, but he did not live to see this great moment in the history of his country. He was assassinated on April 14, 1865, just nine months before the Thirteenth Amendment became the law of the land.

Slavery in the United States no longer exists, because Lincoln and men like him knew that no man is free unless all men are free. And yet, amendments and laws do not guarantee the changes they seek. The people of the United States were not all in agreement about slavery. The War Between the States stands as proof of this disagreement.

1

Let us think back. Many Americans do not know that slavery was a part of American history from the days of the earliest colonial settlements in Virginia. Slavery did not, however, originate in America. For thousands of years, primitive and civilized people, including those in biblical times, have kept slaves. How did we happen to have slaves in the United States? Who were these people? Where did they come from? How did they get here? Who brought them? And for what purpose? And why could not all citizens — both southerners and northerners — agree that slavery must not exist in a free country?

This book answers these questions. This is the story of slavery in the United States of America. This is the story of what has been called "that peculiar institution."

Chapter One

HOW SLAVERY CAME TO THE ENGLISH COLONIES

A young English colonist posted atop a hillside overlooking the harbor of Jamestown, Virginia, suddenly spied a billowing white sail. He searched for some sign of identification and saw that it was a Dutch ship — the one he had been sent to look for. It was sure to be laden with tools, tea, spices, cloth — the necessities of life — and even a few luxuries that the colonists could afford to buy in this year of 1619.

Life was hard in the new land. It was a constant struggle just to produce the food that was needed. There was not much time or money to spend on luxuries, and so the colonists were anxiously awaiting news of the ship's arrival.

The boy ran to alert the villagers, and those who could went down to the harbor to wait for the ship to dock. Soon the goods would be unloaded, and the men would buy whatever they could afford.

A strange sight met their eyes. Not just goods were unloaded, but men — twenty of them. They were tall and handsome. They looked very strong. Their skin was dark — much darker than that of the Indians the colonists had found living in this new land.

Slaves were used to work in the tobacco industry of Virginia.

These men on the ship were black, and they were for sale. They had been taken forcibly from their homes in Africa, and sold to the Dutch by tribal chiefs. They would, in turn, be sold to the colonists at great profit by their Dutch owners. They would be bound to their new owners to work for a period of from five to seven years.

There already were white bound-servants, known as indentured servants, living in Virginia. The contract that bound them was called an indenture because it was "indented," or cut in two; one part was kept by the master and the other part by the servant.

Most of the white indentured servants who had come to Virginia from England were men and women who, because they were unable to pay for their passage to America, had contracted to work in payment for their transportation. They entered into these contracts

4

White slave-traders inspect and buy African slaves.

of their own free will. The men learned to raise crops. Most of the women became maids or dairywomen, although sometimes they worked in the fields with the men. For their work they were usually paid only with food and clothing. They could be sold to others at a profit. They could be given in payment for a debt. They could be transferred like pieces of furniture or cows or horses. When their terms of service had ended, they were sometimes given land or tools or money or seed, and were set free to come and go as they pleased.

The same conditions applied to the twenty Africans who were sold to the English colonists in Jamestown, Virginia, in 1619, just twelve years after the colony had been established. These twenty African indentured servants became America's first Negroes. When they had served their terms, they were freed. Thus the first Negroes

5

Slave owners hunted and trapped slaves trying to escape.

in America gained their freedom from five to seven years after they arrived on the Dutch ship in 1619. Some of these free Negroes obtained land and became farmers; others became artisans and worked for their former masters as carpenters, builders, and workers in iron. And this time, they were paid for their work.

After a while, however, bound or indentured servants became so scarce and the need for them became so great, that other means had to be found to fill the jobs on the colonists' farms and plantations. Servants had to be found who could *not* leave after their terms had expired, who could *not* become free, who could *not* own property, who could *not* become free artisans or skilled workers who could sell their services. The colonists needed perpetual servants who could be treated as possessions to be bought and sold at the convenience of their owners.

This need for cheap and perpetual labor is actually what created the institution of slavery. And there are several reasons why the Negro servants and not the white became slaves. Negroes, unlike the white indentured servants, were considered "foreigners," because they were not English. Negroes, unlike white servants, had been brought to colonies such as Virginia and Maryland against their will. Soon it became the practice *not* to give Negroes the written contract or "indenture." Since Negroes were not English citizens, they could not seek the protection of English law. Runaways could be found easily because of their color. And when white men punished their slaves they felt little or no guilt, for these black men from Africa were not Christians. Some slaves thought they could gain their freedom by being baptized, but laws were passed declaring that conversion did not end their servitude. To establish the Negro's separation from the Europeans, slave

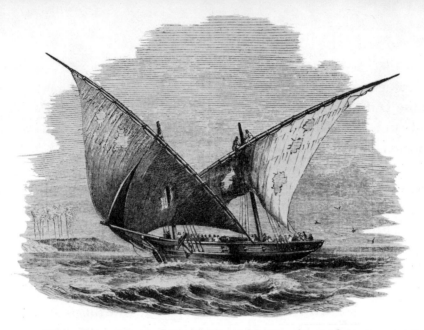

This type of boat, known as a felucca, was used to transport slaves from Africa to the New World.

codes were adopted that made it seem as if the Negro were an "inferior" person.

Beginning in the 1640's, Negroes ceased to be servants and became slaves. Within the next thirty years, they really began to be thought of as property instead of as human beings. In 1661, slavery was legalized in the colony of Virginia. Later, it was legalized in other colonies, and Negroes were imported expressly to become "servants for life"—to become slaves.

By 1700, there were approximately twenty-five thousand Negro slaves in the English colonies. They came on Dutch ships, they came on Spanish ships, on Portuguese ships. During the early 1700's, the British took over the slave trade, with the aid of New England colonial merchants. The slave trade became such a profitable business that some ships carried nothing but slaves.

Chapter Two
SLAVE TRADE AND THE SLAVE MARKETS

As we have seen, in the seventeenth century, during the first period of slavery in the English colonies, the Spanish, Dutch, and Portuguese, as well as the British and the New Englanders, traded actively in slaves. Slavery, however, was growing slowly at this time. Most slaves were in the southern colonies, where cotton, rice, tobacco, and indigo were raised. There were smaller numbers in the middle colonies and in New England.

Most Negroes came to the colonies from West Africa. They represented many different cultures and spoke many different languages and dialects. In their own lands they had lived in small kingdoms, ruled by royal families and tribal leaders. They and their families had lived in small towns or villages or in the interior. Many had been merchants, warriors, farmers, herdsmen, and artisans. Tribal chieftains in Africa were encouraged by the traders to provide a supply of slaves. The chieftains obtained them in various ways, sometimes by kidnapping, sometimes by conquest in their tribal wars. Some Africans were already slaves.

These men and women, obtained by tribal chieftains, and sold to the slave traders, were herded like cattle, chained together, into

9

the dark dungeons of the ships' holds. They were treated like animals — whole families were ill fed, ill clothed, beaten, deprived of their possessions. Many died as a result of this treatment; many jumped overboard long before the voyage was over. Those who lived were broken in spirit, with no will to resist a fate that they could not even imagine. It is little wonder that they arrived in their new land bitter and resentful. And when they were bought and sold like chattel, life became unbearable to them.

Many of the slaves who arrived in the English colonies in the seventeenth century did not come directly from Africa. Traders frequently took slaves from Africa to the West Indies for "training"

This plan of a slave ship shows the inhuman conditions under which slaves were shipped to America.

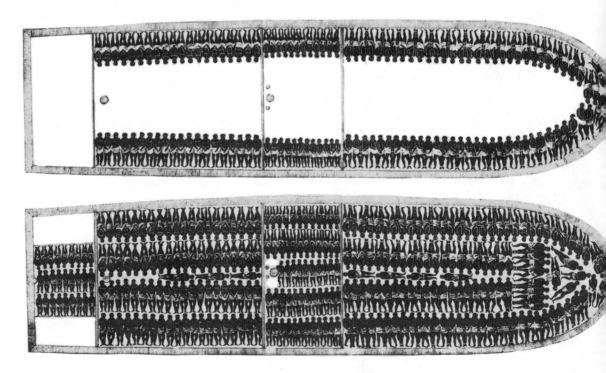

The SUGAR-CANE , SUGAR-MILL, &c.

Slaves at work making sugar in the West Indies.

or "seasoning," before they brought them to the colonies for sale. After 1700, however, the growth of the southern plantations increased the demand for labor, or slaves. As dealing in slaves became more and more profitable, the traders no longer took time to have the slaves "trained" in the West Indies. At the same time, slave owners found that the more educated slaves were not as easy to control as those with no education.

In the days when slaves were still being sent to the West Indies the American traders would transport sugar from the West Indies to New England's rum distilleries, then cross to West Africa, where the rum was exchanged for slaves, and from there to what was called the Middle Passage, back to the New World — to the slave markets.

This was known as Triangular Trade because the route from the West Indies to New England, then to Africa and back to the West Indies was in the form of a triangle.

The traders found this practice very profitable. The result was that their trading increased to the point where in 1707, a hundred years after the founding of Jamestown, Negroes in Virginia numbered 12,000 and were being imported at the rate of about 1,000 a year. By the year 1800, there were 260,000 Negroes in Virginia

Triangular Trade Route. Sugar from the West Indies was sent to New England, where it was used to make rum, which was then taken to West Africa and exchanged for slaves who were brought back to the New World.

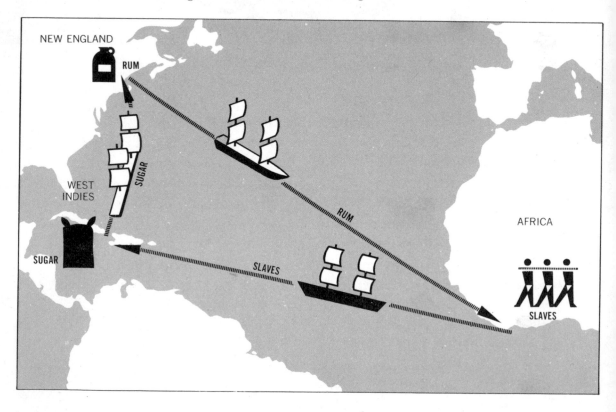

alone. In fact, just before the American Revolution, the number of Negroes and whites in Virginia was about equal.

Slave importations throughout the colonies had increased from an average of 2,500 to 7,500 per year until just before the American Revolution. The increase in the number of slaves, however, does not mean that all of the colonists were in favor of slavery. Some southern plantation owners feared that too many Negroes were being imported and some passed tax laws on the imported slaves. But, the slave traders in both England and New England persuaded the British government to prohibit such taxes. In 1760, South Carolina passed a law to prohibit the slave trade entirely, but again the traders were able to exert enough influence on the English king and his council to prevent the law from taking effect. As a result, slave importation and slave trading went on and became more and more profitable.

When the Constitution went into effect, in 1789, there were four million people in the United States. Of these, about 750,000 were Negro slaves. It was to the tobacco and cotton plantations of Virginia and the rice, cotton, indigo, and sugarcane plantations of the Deep South that most of the slaves were sold. But there were slaves throughout the English colonies and the mainland of America. There were slaves in Maryland, Delaware, and even in Pennsylvania, as well as right up the Atlantic coastline into New York and New England, though here they were not numerous, because north of Virginia the farms were much smaller and fewer slaves were needed. Many slaves, however, became servants in the homes of the rich merchants of the northern colonies.

Slave markets, as they became known, were set up in ports from New England to Virginia. The largest of all during the colonial period was in Newport, Rhode Island.

In Newport, slaves right off the ships were displayed for sale — as families, as groups of men, as groups of women, or as individuals. The buyers would examine them and choose them according to the type of workers they needed and the amount of money they could afford to spend. The slaves were examined as animals would have been examined. The men had to be strong to work in the fields — to sow, to till, and to harvest. They had to be strong to cultivate and work in the forests and to fell the trees. They had to work on the farms and in the villages as barrelmakers, carpenters, blacksmiths. The women would be used as cooks, waitresses, maids, nurses; and the children, as grooms for the horses and cattle or as aids to the men and women picking cotton in the fields.

A northern slave house in New Hampshire.

A sketch of a family for sale at a slave auction in Virginia.

Inside the United States, trading in slaves was a legal business. When cotton growing made the use of slaves essential, new slave markets opened in Baltimore, Richmond, Norfolk, Charleston, Memphis, and New Orleans, and even in Washington, the national

15

BY
HEWLETT & BRIGHT.

SALE OF
VALUABLE
SLAVES,

(On account of departure)

The Owner of the following named and valuable Slaves, being on the eve of departure for Europe, will cause the same to be offered for sale, at the NEW EXCHANGE, corner of St. Louis and Chartres streets, on *Saturday,* May 16, at Twelve o'Clock, *viz.*

1. SARAH, a mulatress, aged 45 years, a good cook and accustomed to house work in general, is an excellent and faithful nurse for sick persons, and in every respect a first rate character.

2. DENNIS, her son, a mulatto, aged 24 years, a first rate cook and steward for a vessel, having been in that capacity for many years on board one of the Mobile packets; is strictly honest, temperate, and a first rate subject.

3. CHOLE, a mulatress, aged 36 years, she is, without execption, one of the most competent servants in the country, a first rate washer and ironer, does up lace, a good cook, and for a bachelor who wishes a house-keeper she would be invaluable; she is also a good ladies' maid, having travelled to the North in that capacity.

4. FANNY, her daughter, a mulatress, aged 16 years, speaks French and English, is a superior hair-dresser, (pupil of Guilliac,) a good seamstress and ladies' maid, is smart, intelligent, and a first rate character.

5. DANDRIDGE, a mulatoo, aged 26 years, a first rate dining-room servant, a good painter and rough carpenter, and has but few equals for honesty and sobriety.

6. NANCY, his wife, aged about 24 years, a confidential house servant, good seamstress, mantuamaker and tailoress, a good cook, washer and ironer, etc.

7. MARY ANN, her child, a creole, aged 7 years, speaks French and English, is smart, active and intelligent.

8. FANNY or FRANCES, a mulatress, aged 22 years, is a first rate washer and ironer, good cook and house servant, and has an excellent character.

9. EMMA, an orphan, aged 10 or 11 years, speaks French and English, has been in the country 7 years, has been accustomed to waiting on table, sewing etc.; is intelligent and active.

10. FRANK, a mulatto, aged about 32 years speaks French and English, is a first rate hostler and coachman, understands perfectly well the management of horses, and is, in every respect, a first rate character, with the exception that he will occasionally drink, though not an habitual drunkard.

☞ All the above named Slaves are acclimated and excellent subjects; they were purchased by their present vendor many years ago, and will, therefore, be severally warranted against all vices and maladies prescribed by law, save and except FRANK, who is fully guaranteed in every other respect but the one above mentioned.

TERMS:—One-half Cash, and the other half in notes at Six months, drawn and endorsed to the satisfaction of the Vendor, with special mortgage on the Slaves until final payment. The Acts of Sale to be passed before WILLIAM BOSWELL, *Notary Public*, at the expense of the Purchaser.

New-Orleans, May 13, 1835.

PRINTED BY BENJAMIN LEVY.

Announcement of a New Orleans slave sale in 1835.

Slaves were sometimes branded like cattle.

capital. The slaves were brought to these additional markets by coastal vessels, river steamboats, or they were transported overland, fastened together with chains or ropes. Slave traders bought and sold the slaves as they would have bought and sold cattle. In these new markets, the slaves were subjected to even greater indignities than in Newport. As they stood on the platform during a sale, they were touched, poked, examined, inspected, and made to jump up and down to test their strength.

After the viewing, came the bidding. The slaves were sold to the highest bidder. The most expensive slave, a field hand, or as he was called, a prime field hand, ranged in age from eighteen to twenty-

17

five and cost from five hundred dollars in 1832, to eighteen hundred dollars just before the Civil War. The cost of keeping a slave varied from about fifteen to sixty dollars per year. The slaves were sold not only as families, but also as individuals, for families were broken up to suit the needs or finances of the bidders.

One story is told of a mother and her two children, a boy and a girl. The father had already been sold. Later the rest of the family was also put up for sale. When a buyer purchased the young boy, the mother pleaded with him to buy them all, but he could not afford to. The mother burst into tears and the slave trader turned to her with his whip and threatened to beat her if she did not stop her noise. As the little boy turned to go with his new owner, he said, sadly, "Don't cry, mama. I will be a good boy. Don't cry." After the American Revolution, only two states prohibited the separation of children from their families and then only if they were under ten years of age. The poet John Greenleaf Whittier wrote this sad song of a mother whose child had been taken from her.

> Gone, gone — sold and gone
> To the rice-swamp, dank and lone . . .

Chapter Three
LIFE ON THE PLANTATION

Perhaps you have heard that "most slave owners were good to their slaves." There are two things wrong with such a statement. First, brutality toward slaves was a common practice. Second, even the kind slave owners were not "good," for no amount of good treatment can justify denying a man his freedom.

In America, slaves were generally plantation workers. Since most of the plantations were in the South, most of the slaves were there. The southerners called slavery a peculiar institution, and it surely was. The more slaves a master had, the more it profited him. Slaves were regarded as property, to be bought and sold and used at will. For the plantation owners, slave-owning was a way to obtain wealth. While some owners had only a few slaves, others had a hundred or more, depending upon the size of the farm or plantation.

As the number of slaves in the South grew larger, the masters began to fear slave uprisings. They also feared that the slaves might conspire with the Indians. That is why the colonists decided to enact slave codes. Their slaves were not allowed to learn to read or write, they were not allowed off the plantations, their marriages were not considered legal, they could be separated from their families, and for minor offenses, slaves could be branded with a hot iron, flogged, beaten, and even killed.

Let us imagine that we are on a southern plantation, seeing what life was like for both the owner and the slave.

Plantations were usually located on the banks of a river so that goods could be more easily shipped to the coast. Their size varied — some were just a few acres and had just a few slaves, while others ranged from a hundred to a thousand acres. Small holdings often were merged to form large plantations. The owners would not usually abuse their slaves, for how could an injured slave work? But, as the plantations became larger, overseers were employed to manage them. The overseers, who had to get the greatest amount of work out of the slaves, were often harsh and cruel.

A painting of a southern cotton plantation. (MUSEUM OF FINE ARTS, BOSTON; M. AND M. KAROLIK COLLECTION)

FREDERICK DOUGLASS TELLS ABOUT FOOD AND CLOTHING AS A SLAVE

Frederick Douglass, who was born a slave and eventually escaped, described the food and clothing slaves received:

The men and women slaves on Colonel Lloyd's farm received their monthly allowance of food . . . eight pounds of pickled pork or its equivalent in fish . . . with their pork or fish, they had given them one bushel of Indian meal. . . . The yearly allowance of clothing was not more ample than the supply of food. . . . Children under ten years old had neither shoes, stockings, jackets, nor trousers (pants). They had two . . . shirts per year, and when they were worn out, they went naked till next allowance day. . . .

The large planters lived in handsome houses, comfortably and often luxuriously furnished, with great lawns, landscaped gardens, and fine verandas, where, waited upon by their house slaves, they could sit in comfort and enjoy cool drinks. They had plenty of good food and fine clothing. They had plenty of time for recreation and visiting their neighbors, for hunting and fishing. They gave and attended elaborate parties throughout the South, and some traveled to Europe. They shopped for stylish clothes in Charleston or in New Orleans. Their children had private tutors and went to fine schools in this country and in England.

Slaves around their owner's house in South Carolina.

House slaves were often nursemaids for their owners' children.

On the large plantations, some of the house slaves cleaned, sewed, took care of the children, cooked, and served the food to the family, while others worked on the lawns and the flower or vegetable gardens. Still other slaves worked as butlers, carpenters, blacksmiths, brickmakers, stonemasons, weavers, or shoemakers. Many became highly skilled. In other words, the slaves made life very enjoyable for their masters. These house slaves, who became the butlers, the maids, the valets, the nursemaids, or artisans, were usually adequately fed and clothed. Their masters often became very fond of their slaves and proud of their skills. The slaves, in turn, often took on some of the fine manners that they saw around them.

But what of the slaves who worked in the fields? They literally "slaved" from early dawn to sunset, in the broiling sun, sometimes without either adequate food or water during their working hours. Some slaves lived with their own families in cabins on the plantation and were fairly well treated. Most, however, lived in miserable shacks, ate inadequate food at hours convenient to the working demands, and were often separated from their families. They had little, if any, medical care and, on the average, did not live very long.

They were not happy and carefree, as we have sometimes been led to believe. They did not sing and dance to the extent that we have come to think that they did. They may have seemed content, on the surface. But, more often than not, there was a quiet, sometimes bitter resignation to their fate. They might have pretended to be happy, but deep down they felt a sadness that comes out very clearly in their songs.

Field slaves picking cotton worked long hours.

Here are a few examples of their songs. Read the words carefully, and then decide for yourself whether or not they are happy and carefree.

TROUBLE

Trouble, trouble, trouble,
Done had trouble all my days,
Trouble, trouble, trouble,
Done had trouble all my days.
Seems, boys, like dese troubles
Gwine to carry me to my grave.

MARCH ON

Way over in Egypt's land
You shall gain the victory.
This is the year of jubilee,
You gwine to gain the victory,
Old Moses set his people free
You gwine to gain the day.
March on, Lawd, and you will gain the victory;
March, my brother, Lawd, and you gwine gain the day.
We need no cowards in our band,
We call for valiant-hearted men.

BETTER DAY A-COMING

There's a better day a-coming, Hallelujah!
For we don't feel no ways tired,
O chilluns Hallelujah!
We all shout, Glory! Shout Freedom!
O, glory Hallelujah!

Phillis Wheatley, who rose from slavery to become a famous poet, read her poems before nobility in England.

Now read this extract from a poem by Phillis Wheatley, a young slave who had been born in Africa and purchased by a Boston tailor whose family treated her well and provided her with an education. Before the Revolution Phillis took a trip to England, where some of her poems were published. Returning to Boston, free, she married another freed slave in 1784, and wrote her most famous poem, "Liberty and Peace." These are the final lines of the poem:

> Auspicious Heaven shall fill with fav'ring Gales
> Where e'er Columbia spreads her swelling sails,
> To every Realm shall peace her charms display
> And Heavenly Freedom spread her Golden Day.

26

When you read the words of the songs and the poem, you can see how they are filled with hope and despair. If you could hear the melodies of the songs, you would find them sad and mournful. These works reflect the fact that although the slaves were religious, they were so only because they looked forward to a better life after death, for there was not much hope of a good life here on earth.

But, suddenly, before the end of the eighteenth century, a strange thing began to happen on the southern plantations. It was something that might have ended slavery without any laws or rebellions. It might have made slavery a very minor issue in the Civil War.

Many slaves lived in small, overcrowded cabins or shacks.

BOOKER T. WASHINGTON TELLS ABOUT LIFE AS A SLAVE

This is how Booker T. Washington, in his autobiography, describes his childhood as an ex-slave:

I cannot remember having slept in a bed until after our family was declared free by the Emancipation Proclamation.

Great numbers of slaves were used in the production of cotton.

One day, as he was looking over his accounts, a southern planter noticed that it was costing him more money to keep his slaves than they were earning for him. Orders from England for his cotton had decreased. They continued to decrease and profits began to fall still more. What could he do about this? Get rid of his slaves? Go into another business? It was a problem.

The problem was solved without any effort on the part of the plantation owner and with no change in the status of the slaves. The solution made slavery more vital than ever to the economy of the South. Machinery to do the work of spinning the cotton into cloth was developed in England, and the orders for southern cotton began to come in so fast that it was hard to keep up with them. What we call the Industrial Revolution was under way. After it began in England in the middle of the eighteenth century, slaves became even more important than they had been before. In some cases more and more slaves had to be bought to fill the orders for cotton.

One problem in working with cotton had been solved — how to get rid of the cotton that was produced. But it took a slave a full day to prepare one single pound of clean cotton fiber by hand. So the plantation owners were faced with this problem of removing the seeds from the cotton fiber, and meeting the increase in orders from England and the North.

Then a New England schoolteacher, Eli Whitney, invented a machine called the cotton gin, which made it possible for ten pounds of cotton to be cleaned in the time it had previously taken to clean one pound. When the cotton gin was used with a horse and water, the production rate was raised to as high as a thousand pounds per man per day.

Now both problems were solved. The production of cotton

UNITED STATES COTTON PRODUCTION

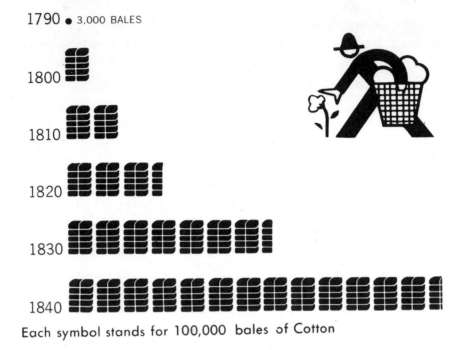

1790 ● 3,000 BALES

1800

1810

1820

1830

1840

Each symbol stands for 100,000 bales of Cotton

needed more and more slaves to plant, cultivate, and harvest the cotton, as well as to clean the cotton itself. The wealth of the southern planter, the New England shipper, the English textile manufacturer, the Yankee millowner and the merchant were completely dependent upon the slave labor of American Negroes.

In 1792, before Whitney invented the cotton gin, the United States produced relatively few bales of cotton. In 1840, over 1,300,000 bales of cotton were grown. (One bale weighs five hundred pounds.) Cotton was king and slavery was tied more solidly onto the South. Cotton plantations expanded into Alabama, Mississippi, and Louisiana, and slaves were needed more than ever. Although the Constitution forbade the importation of slaves after

1808, some 300,000 were smuggled into the United States from Africa between 1808 and 1861, when the Civil War began. In order to increase the supply of slaves, some owners encouraged their slaves to have children who could be sold into slavery. And there were instances where free Negroes were kidnapped and made slaves.

There was no thought of ending slavery as a matter of saving money. Quite the opposite was true — the entire business life and earning power of the South seemed to depend upon keeping the practice as a permanent institution. Besides, people were moving into territories in the West, where their businesses and farms needed slave labor. As a result of the greater and greater demand for cotton and the opening of the new western territories, the

With the invention of the cotton gin, more cotton could be cleaned in less time.

GINNING COTTON BY STEAM

Unloading the slave cargo from a vessel captured after slave trade was out-lawed.

owners demanded more and more production from their slaves. They ordered them to work even longer hours, under the same conditions. The slaves became more dissatisfied and rebellious. They were ready to listen to any plan or any person who could promise to get them away from their intolerable life. They wanted to be free, and for freedom they were willing to risk their lives.

32

Chapter Four
A MOVEMENT STARTS TO FREE THE SLAVES

Slavery had become an issue in America even before the Revolution. Some of the colonists who were struggling against what they called their slavery to England began working to free the slaves in America. Crispus Attucks, a runaway slave, was one of the first to die in the struggle. The legend of his bravery at the Boston Massacre was so inspiring that it increased public support for a movement to end slavery.

Revolutionary leaders felt that they could not demand freedom for themselves, if they denied freedom to the Negroes. Among these men were James Otis, Thomas Paine, Thomas Jefferson, and Benjamin Franklin. They believed that no one had the right to own another human being. Benjamin Franklin had organized a society in Pennsylvania to abolish slavery. Another of the great leaders of the Revolution was Patrick Henry. He had made a speech in which he had said, "Give me liberty, or give me death." This speech inspired many of those who were opposed to slavery. Thomas Jefferson and a prominent minister, Isaac Skillman, had shown that slavery was wrong and had left provisions in their wills to free their slaves. Later, George Washington put the same clause in his will.

THE FATE OF A RUNAWAY SLAVE

In 1854, a runaway slave named Anthony Burns was living in Boston. He was very happy there, and had found a good life among the Bostonians.

When his master, a Virginia slave owner, discovered where he was, he demanded that Burns be returned to Virginia. Burns was arrested and put into chains. Many people tried to have him released. Meetings were held in Faneuil Hall, and Wendell Phillips and Richard H. Dana, Jr., came to him to help him. Phillips was one of the most prominent abolitionists and Dana was a well-known lawyer.

An attempt was made to take the prisoner by force. A crowd stormed the courthouse and broke in the door. A hundred men were guarding Burns. They beat a Negro who was trying to help Burns, and one of the guards was killed. Marines were sent from the Navy Yard and soldiers from Fort Independence. Rioters were arrested by Boston police.

Even from the surrounding towns, people came to join the protest against the imprisonment of Burns. One night, when Dana was on his way home, he was attacked by one of the guards.

At the trial, Dana pleaded for the release of Burns, but he was not successful. The unfortunate Burns was ordered returned to his master in Virginia.

He was put on board a Naval vessel, under a large police and military guard. The ship was ordered out by President Franklin Pierce for the purpose of returning Anthony Burns to slavery.

Jefferson had written a clause condemning slavery in his draft of the Declaration of Independence. This passage was taken out of the final version, as a result of pressures from the southern states and one northern state — Rhode Island. Nevertheless, the Declaration of Independence did say that "... all men are created equal, that they are endowed by their Creator with certain unalienable Rights, that among these are Life, Liberty and the pursuit of Happiness." Although these words do, in fact, condemn slavery, some people refused to admit that this was what was meant.

During the American Revolution, although Negroes were not at first allowed in the Army, General George Washington later

Two Negroes, Oliver Cromwell and Prince Whipple, were with George Washington when he crossed the Delaware.

During the Revolution, Peter Salem (right) fought in the Battle of Bunker
Hill.

changed his mind about this. Eventually some five thousand Negroes served in the Continental Army. Slaves distinguished themselves at Lexington, Concord, and Yorktown; Bunker Hill had two Negro heroes, Peter Salem and Salem Poor. When General Washington crossed the Delaware River, two Negroes, Oliver Cromwell and Prince Whipple, were with him. A Negro spy named Pompey secured the information that enabled General Anthony Wayne to recapture the American fort at Stony Point in 1779.

After the Revolutionary War, slaves who had been with the Army were freed. What was to be done with these freed slaves? An organization called the American Colonization Society was formed in 1817 to find a solution. The Society bought some land in what is today the African country of Liberia, and proposed that the free Negroes be sent there as settlers. Congress, however, refused to pay the high cost of transportation, and many whites and free Negroes opposed the plan. However, in the peak year of the plan, eight hundred Negroes managed to get to Liberia, but many could not adjust to this new land; others became ill and died. The plan was abandoned, but not the desire to find some solution to the problem of slavery and of the freed Negro in American society.

Following the Revolution the surveyed boundary between the North and the South, called the Mason-Dixon Line after the two men who had done the surveying, served to separate free and slave states. The seven states above the line, which was between Pennsylvania and Maryland, forbade slavery. Those below the line permitted slavery.

A few years after the American Revolution, Congress, operating under the Articles of Confederation, passed the Northwest Ordinance and voted that slavery should never exist in that part of the

Gilbert Hunt, a Virginia slave freed
for his heroism during a Richmond
fire in 1811, attempted to settle in
Liberia but returned to Richmond.

American West north of the Ohio River. And so, when Ohio,
Indiana, Illinois, Michigan, and Wisconsin came into the Union,
they came in as free states. But this same legislation permitted new
states in the South to have slaves. And, this clearly marked off a
free region and a slave region. It was a situation that was sure to
make trouble, and it certainly did as new states came into the
Union, some free and some slave.

The Constitution, which replaced the Articles of Confederation
in 1788, does not contain the word "slavery." According to the
Constitution, "Importation of such Persons as any of the States . . .
[thought] proper to admit . . . [was not to be] prohibited . . . prior
to the year one thousand eight hundred and eight. . . ." This meant
that the slave trade would be allowed to continue for twenty years.
The Constitution also provided for the return of runaway slaves

and, as a further concession to the South, it permitted five slaves to be counted as three persons in the determination of representation in Congress. In 1820, Congress permitted Missouri, part of the Louisiana Territory, to enter the Union as a slave state but declared the rest of the territory north of it (36° 30′) to be free. This plan was called the Missouri Compromise.

If we look at a map, we see that there were good reasons for the differences in the opinions of northerners and southerners. In the warm climate of the South, cotton, rice, tobacco, and indigo grew well, and for this reason, southerners found their "peculiar institution" of slavery profitable. They said that since the northern states did not need this form of labor, they could afford to disapprove of slavery.

In fact, while slavery was becoming more important in the agricultural South, free labor was becoming more important in the industrial North. And time and time again the slavery issue would divide the country. By the middle of the nineteenth century over 90 per cent of the slaves lived on the plantations and farms of the South. Only 10 per cent of the slaves were living in the towns and cities of the South. The town slaves did menial work in homes and shops and often hard labor with a pick and a shovel. Sometimes the planters allowed their slaves to work in the towns during the slow season on the plantations. There they could learn to be carpenters, shoemakers, painters, and mechanics. When they came back to the plantations they were more valuable, for they could use their newly learned skills on the plantations. If they were offered for sale, they would bring much more money than a simple field worker. But, even as far back as then, white workers were not happy about teaching Negroes a trade, because they were afraid that their own jobs might be in danger. They contended

The southern view of slavery. The master, relaxing, says to his slave: "My boy — we've toiled and taken care of you long enough — now you've got to work."

A free Negro working in New York.

Northern factories employed free laborers rather than slaves.

Abolitionist William Lloyd Garrison.

that the Negroes were not intelligent enough to learn a trade, in spite of the large number of Negroes working in the cotton mills, sawmills, iron furnaces, and tobacco factories, and operating complicated factory and dock machinery that required considerable skill.

While the slaves who lived in the towns had more freedom than those on the farms and plantations, their lives were still very restricted. They were required to report for work at a certain time and to return to their homes after work and remain there until it was time to leave for work the next morning.

The slaves' dissatisfaction grew as their numbers increased. At the same time, there arose throughout the country stronger and stronger feelings against slavery. The antislavery movement began to gain momentum.

Many articles were written by both white and Negro journalists, calling upon the Negroes to rise up and rebel against slavery and slave owners. The term "abolitionist" became the common name for all those, both black and white, who wanted to do away with slavery. The antislavery movement became known as the abolitionist movement; in other words, the movement to do away with slavery.

Frederick Douglass, famous writer, editor, and abolitionist.

Among the most famous advocates of freedom for the slaves was a white newspaperman named William Lloyd Garrison. Garrison's articles against slavery were read all over the country. In his newspaper, the *Liberator,* he announced, "I determine at every hazard, to lift up the standard of emancipation.... That standard is now unfurled; and long may it float ... till every chain be broken, and every bondsman be free." Garrison and his abolitionists held conventions, published articles, sent out speakers to collect funds, and asked all people who believed in freedom to join them. Men and women, both whites and Negroes, answered the call. Some planters even set their slaves free and went North to join in this movement.

Of all the Negro abolitionists, Frederick Douglass was the most famous. He had been born a slave in Maryland, but had escaped at the age of twenty-one and joined the abolitionists. He became a great orator and writer, and one of the most eloquent of the abolitionist spokesmen. He made many enemies and had to flee to Europe to escape death. After a few years, Douglass returned to America, bought his freedom, and became the editor of an antislavery newspaper in Rochester, New York. His paper, the *North Star,* and his autobiography, *My Bondage and My Freedom,* were among the most widely read antislavery writings of the period. During his entire life as a free man, Douglass continued his antislavery work. During the Civil War he helped to raise Negro troops. He worked throughout his life for emancipation and for civil rights. To this day, he is revered as one of the greatest exponents of the rights of all men.

Another former slave who was a powerful speaker for abolition was a woman named Sojourner Truth. Tall and very thin, with a deep and impressive voice and a quick mind, she spoke of her own experiences as a slave. Her audiences were so impressed by her that

Sojourner Truth, an influential spokesman against slavery.

they never forgot what she said. On one occasion, when another speaker praised the Constitution, Sojourner Truth said that it reminded her of some wheat stalks that looked very big, but had no wheat in them. The reason there was no wheat, she said, was that a little "weasel" was in the stalks. What she meant was that there was a little weevil, an insect that ate away the wheat. And, she said, that when she picked up the Constitution, it seemed very big and strong, but when she felt for her rights there were no rights there. What was wrong with the Constitution? It too had "a little 'weasel' in it."

Abolitionists in both the North and the South organized what was called the Underground Railroad. This was not really a railroad, for it had no tracks or trains, or passengers, in the ordinary sense of the words. The railroad was a plan to help Negroes escape from the South to safety in the North. The Negroes would leave their cabins in the dark of the night. They were the "passengers." Their leaders, both Negro and white, were the "conductors." Their only guide was the North Star, located by the Big Dipper, which they called the Drinking Gourd. The houses or "stations" where runaway slaves could hide along the way had drinking gourds hanging outside to identify them as safe places for shelter or for help.

There is even a song about the "drinking gourd." It goes:

Follow, follow the drinking gourd.
Follow, follow the drinking gourd,
For the old man is a-waitin'
For to carry you to freedom.
Follow, follow the drinking gourd.

The most famous and celebrated Negro "conductor" of the Underground Railroad was a former slave named Harriet Tubman who had escaped north from Maryland when she was twenty-five years old. When she heard of the Underground Railroad, she joined the abolitionists. She journeyed to the South at least twenty times and led more than three hundred men and women from slavery to freedom, risking her own life many times. Once, forty thousand dollars was offered for her capture, but she was never caught and not one of her passengers was ever lost. Harriet Tubman risked her life again as a scout for the Union troops during the Civil War.

Slaves escaping to freedom.

Harriet Tubman, best-known "conductor" of the Underground Railroad, guided slaves as far north as Canada to gain their freedom.

Harriet Beecher Stowe, author of *Uncle Tom's Cabin*.

Among the many whites who fought bravely for abolition were two young southern women, the Grimké sisters, who had been born on a large plantation. Early in their lives they had joined the abolitionists and had made speeches against slavery everywhere they were asked to speak. One of them married Theodore Weld, a leading abolitionist.

Harriet Beecher Stowe wrote a story for a Washington newspaper, which became known as *Uncle Tom's Cabin*. Mrs. Stowe's story described the hard life of the slaves on the plantations. She told of the relations between the masters and the slaves, and of the cruelty of the overseers. She had not lived in the South, but she had gained her knowledge from stories told to her by slaves who had sought refuge in her home in Cincinnati, which had been a "station" on the Underground Railroad. The book relates the suffering of the slaves Uncle Tom and Eliza, and the cruelty of the overseer Simon Legree. *Uncle Tom's Cabin* was denounced in the South, but the more it was denounced there, the more it was be-

HOW ONE SLAVE BECAME FREE AND SUCCESSFUL

Ayuba Suleiman, a member of an upper-class family living in the Senegal River area of Africa, had been a successful merchant when he was captured in 1730. He was made a slave and was sent to America where he was bought by a slave owner in Maryland. He was sent to work on a tobacco plantation. While he was working there, he was noticed by some Englishmen who were visiting the plantation.

The Englishmen were so impressed by Suleiman's appearance and his manner that they secured his freedom. They took him to England, where he was presented to the royal family. These same Englishmen made it possible for Suleiman to go back into business in West Africa, where he was able to make contacts with nearby English traders.

Suleiman once again became a successful merchant, through the efforts and assistance of these Englishmen and their associates.

lieved in the North. The story was also made into a stirring play that moved many people to tears as they watched Eliza being chased by hounds while trying to escape from slavery. *Uncle Tom's Cabin* won more people over to the cause of antislavery than any other single piece of writing or event. Abraham Lincoln once said the book was among the causes of the Civil War.

One of the things that had led Mrs. Stowe to write *Uncle Tom's Cabin* had been the reaction of the abolitionists to the Fugitive

Slave Law. With the enactment of this law, a slave who had run away could be brought into a Federal court. He could not defend himself and he could not have a jury trial. If the court ruled that he was still a slave, he could be returned to his master. According to the Fugitive Slave Law, anyone who even helped a slave to escape could be imprisoned and fined. But the abolitionists defied this law when it was necessary to protect a runaway and many helped the slaves to escape to Canada, where a new settlement of escaped slaves was established. The abolitionists published articles against the Fugitive Slave Law. One of the most prominent of these antislavery publishers was the Reverend Charles Beecher, a brother of Harriet Beecher Stowe.

Chapter Five
SLAVE REBELLIONS AND THE FREE NEGROES

There was a common feeling among the slaves in America — they longed for freedom. Most of them seemed to be peaceful and obedient, but they really had no choice, and deep inside many were restless and resentful. It was easy to convince them to take action to gain their freedom. Almost from the beginning of slavery there were slaves who rebelled against the cruelty of their masters and the harshness of the slave codes.

The first uprising was in the colony of Virginia during the latter part of the seventeenth century. Although the rebellion was put down, the slaves were not discouraged. In 1739, a rebellion known as the Cato conspiracy was organized in South Carolina. It, too, failed. Even though they were not successful and though many whites and Negroes lost their lives, these early rebellions against slavery gave hope to the slaves.

Just as there were slaves in the North as well as in the South, there were rebellions in both the North and the South. In New York, before the Revolutionary War, whites and slaves joined together to set fire to a building. The militia was called out and many of the rebels were killed. Some of the rebels even chose to take their own lives rather than be captured. Not long after this, New York City experienced a series of unexplained fires. Harsh laws had been passed to control Negroes in New York, and it was believed that these fires had been set by poor whites and Negroes who wanted to gain control of the city. There was panic, and even though there was not much evidence against them, more than 150 people, including 25 whites, were seized and tried. In all, 101 Negroes were convicted — 13 were burned alive, 18 were hanged, and 70 were expelled from the colony. The public was so hysterical that it was impossible to hold a fair trial.

Of the uprisings that went on into the nineteenth century, three stand out as examples of bravery and devotion to the cause of freedom among the slaves. The first of these, Gabriel's Revolt, took place in 1800. Gabriel Prosser was a thirty-four-year-old slave on a plantation near Richmond, Virginia. He organized thousands of slaves, armed them, and planned to attack the city of Richmond. But the authorities were informed before the outbreak, and the state militia stopped the rebelling slaves. Many escaped, but of those captured, thirty-six, including Gabriel, were executed. One slave told his captors that, like the soldiers in the Revolution, he too was willing to give his life to help his fellow slaves.

Denmark Vesey, another leader of a slave revolt, had been a slave in South Carolina. He had purchased his freedom and had become a successful carpenter. He learned to read and write and to speak several languages. For a number of years, he carefully planned what came to be known as Vesey's Rebellion (1822). He selected his "troops" among the slaves, appointed his "lieutenants," and collected weapons, which he hid in secret caves. He prepared disguises for his "army" in what amounted to a true cloak-and-dagger plot. But, again there were informers, and again the authorities suc-

The capture of Nat Turner, leader of the most famous of all slave rebellions.

ceeded in crushing the plot. Some have estimated that Vesey had gathered together an organization of over nine thousand Negroes. More than a hundred were arrested, and forty-seven were executed.

The slave owners worried. They passed harsher laws to prevent their slaves from rebelling. But, in 1831 came the most famous of all the rebellions — the Turner Rebellion, the largest and most violent of them all. Nat Turner, the leader, was a Virginia slave who, with his fellow conspirators, roamed through the Virginia countryside and killed more than sixty whites. State and Federal troops killed over a hundred Negroes during the fighting. More were captured and hanged. Nat Turner made a dramatic escape into the woods, hiding in caves and in the underbrush. But he, too, was finally tracked down by the authorities and executed.

By this time, white southerners were really frightened. Instead of being convinced that slavery was wrong, they decided to pass stronger laws to restrict the slaves and to end the freeing of individual slaves, under any conditions. This only increased the number of slave uprisings in the South and placed the free Negroes in danger of losing whatever freedom they had, no matter how they had gained it.

What was it like to be a free Negro? It is true that the first Negroes who were brought to Virginia were indentured servants and were set free after their period of service. It is true that some slaves could buy their freedom from their masters. It is true that many were given freedom without payment. It is true that after the Revolution and after the War of 1812, Negroes who had been in the army were given freedom. It is true that as northern states provided for gradual abolition of slavery, many more slaves were

Black and white abolitionists are expelled from a meeting hall in Boston.

Antislavery meetings attended by both blacks and whites were frequently held on Boston Common.

freed. But, as long as they were considered by the slave owners not as free men, but as "free persons of color," free Negroes could not expect to enjoy the privileges of other free men. According to those who approved of slavery, even a free Negro did not deserve freedom.

Still, there were numbers of free Negroes in the eastern counties of Virginia and Maryland, in many of the large cities of the Deep South, including New Orleans. Most of the free Negroes lived in the northern states — in large cities, such as Boston, New York, Cincinnati, and Philadelphia — though some did go into the west and into communities in South Carolina and Florida.

56

Slavery had gradually disappeared in the North following the American Revolution. Individual states acted independently. Vermont, for example, forbade slavery, while other northern states provided for gradual emancipation. The Massachusetts Supreme Court ruled that slavery violated the provision of the state constitution which had stated that "all men are born free and equal."

To southerners, the very presence of free Negroes in their midst was a threat and they took steps to prevent them from influencing

Church service on a southern plantation.

the slaves. As far back as 1793, Virginia had forbidden free Negroes to enter the state. Soon most of the slave states and even some of the free states adopted similar rules. Free Negroes in many states were forbidden to carry arms or to hold meetings without a special license. Like the slaves, the free Negroes could not conduct church services unless a white minister was present. In several states they were prohibited from visiting their relatives or friends, and they could not hold good jobs or own a business which might compete with whites.

Free Negroes had been given the right to vote in some of the original southern states, but the slave states that entered the Union after the Revolution denied Negroes this right. After 1800, more and more states in both the North and the South barred free Negroes from voting. The children of free Negroes, along with those of the slaves, were not allowed to go to public schools, although their families were taxed, and part of their tax money supported public education. In spite of all this, the free Negroes did not fail in their duty to their country. In the War of 1812, at the Battle of Lake Erie, Captain Oliver Perry, the famous hero of that battle, gave citations to Negro sailors who had shown unusual bravery. And, at the Battle of New Orleans, General Andrew Jackson found his two corps of Negro volunteers among the bravest of his entire force. In a letter to the governor of Louisiana, General Jackson highly praised his Negro troops.

Strange as it may seem, after demonstrating their bravery and proving their reliability, free Negroes were barred from enlisting in the armed forces. In the Navy, where a small number of them remained, new regulations were passed restricting the number of Negroes to one-twentieth of the crew of any ship. Negroes were not recruited for service again until the Civil War.

Although few Negroes were allowed to serve in the Navy, many worked on nonmilitary ships.

The majority of the free Negroes lived in poverty, for they could not get good jobs and they could not take part in civic affairs. Most could not get a good education, even in an elementary school. As far as higher education was concerned, there was very little opportunity for Negroes to get far in this country. Some had to go to Europe to get the education that was denied them in their own land. A university in Germany granted a minister's degree to the renowned Reverend James Pennington, and one in Scotland gave

The Reverend James Pennington, who received his Doctor of Divinity Degree from the University of Heidelberg in Germany, wrote about Negro history and preached against slavery.

a doctor's degree to Dr. James Smith. Finally, after Amherst College gave a degree to Edward Jones and Bowdoin College granted one to John B. Russworm, the number of free Negroes admitted into colleges in the United States began to increase. But, this increase was very slow indeed.

Of the free Negroes who did manage to get an education of some sort, many became poets and writers and were among the leading authors of articles, books, and pamphlets against slavery. In the nineteenth century, a free Negro named Ira Aldridge, who studied at what was called the African Free School in New York and later at the University of Glasgow, became a leading actor on the London stage and toured Europe, performing before kings and queens.

There were a few free Negroes who were able to get enough edu-

Ira Aldridge in the title role of Shakespeare's *Othello*.

cation or experience to become inventors. One, Lewis Temple, a blacksmith, invented a harpoon that is still in use today. Another free Negro, Norbert Rillieux, who was from New Orleans, but who was educated in France, invented machines to speed up the processing of sugar.

One of the most talented and capable of the American Negroes who became prominent following the inauguration of George Washington as President was Benjamin Banneker. Banneker had been able to attend a private integrated school in his native Baltimore, and had become interested in science and mathematics. In the 1790's he published an annual almanac that was read by thousands of people. After he had successfully predicted an eclipse of the sun, he attracted the attention of Thomas Jefferson. Jefferson suggested that Washington appoint Banneker to assist in drawing up the plans for the city of Washington. This was such a great honor that soon all of Banneker's writings began to attract attention. The best of these were on world peace and included a special program of educating American children to further the ideals of peace.

But to be a free Negro did not guarantee a man the rights and privileges that came with freedom. Had they been given humane treatment and opportunity, Negroes, both free and slave, would have made even greater contributions to American life and culture. Slavery deprived the Negroes of what the Declaration of Independence had promised to all men — life, liberty, and the pursuit of happiness.

The history of slavery in America proves that no laws can put an end to men's desire for freedom, either for themselves or for others. The slaves hoped that their rebellions would convince southerners that slavery was wrong. It had just the opposite effect. All it did was to draw together all those in the South to defend

Benjamin Banneker helped draw up the plans for the city of Washington, D.C.

Banneker's *Almanack* was published annually for several years.

Benjamin Bannicker's
PENNSYLVANIA, DELAWARE,
MARYLAND and VIRGINIA

Almanack

A N D

EPHEMERIS,
FOR THE YEAR OF OUR LORD,

1 7 9 2;

Being BISSEXTILE, or LEAP-YEAR, and the SIX-
TEENTH YEAR of AMERICAN INDEPENDENCE,
which commenced *July* 4, 1776.
CONTAINING, the Motions of the Sun and Moon, the true
Places and Aspects of the Planets, the Rising and Setting of
the Sun, and the Rising, Setting and Southing, Place and Age
of the Moon, &c.—The Lunations, Conjunctions, Eclipses,
Judgment of the Weather, Festivals, and other remarkable
Days; Days for holding the Supreme and Circuit Courts of the
United States, as also the usual Courts in *Pennsylvania, Delaware, Maryland,* and *Virginia.*—ALSO, several useful Tables,
and valuable Receipts.—Various Selections from the Com-
monplace-Book of the *Kentucky Philosopher,* an *American Sage;*
with interesting and entertaining Essays, in Prose and Verse—
the whole comprising a greater, more pleasing, and useful Va-
riety, than any Work of the *Kind* and *Price* in *North-America.*

BALTIMORE: Printed and Sold, Wholesale and Retail, by
WILLIAM GODDARD and JAMES ANGELL, at their Print-
ing-Office, in *Market-Street.*—Sold, also, by Mr. JOSEPH
CRUKSHANK, Printer, in *Market-Street,* and Mr. DANIEL
HUMPHREYS, Printer, in *South-Front-Street, Philadelphia;*
and by Messrs. HANSON and BOND, Printers, in *Alexandria.*

their "peculiar institution." Southerners were so frightened that they enacted harsher laws against both the slaves and the free Negroes. But, also drawn together were organized whites and Negroes who were devoted to the cause of ending slavery through the abolitionist movement.

Chapter Six
SLAVERY AND THE CIVIL WAR

A Compromise Is Broken and a New Party Is Formed

In 1854, a strange quarrel arose in the United States as a result of a bill introduced in Congress by Senator Stephen A. Douglas of Illinois. Douglas wanted to make it possible for settlers west of the Missouri River to have a territorial government. The territory involved was to be divided in two — one part was to be named Kansas, and the land to the north of that would be called Nebraska. Douglas proposed a law that would enable the people of Kansas and of Nebraska to decide for themselves whether or not they wanted slavery. This law, called the Kansas-Nebraska Act, was passed.

Northerners were angered by the law, for they claimed it reversed the Missouri Compromise, which had prohibited slavery in new states. They held meetings in Wisconsin and Michigan and decided to organize a new political party. One of their key objectives would be to fight the extension of slavery into new states. They called their party the Republican party.

In Nebraska there were no problems, but serious difficulties arose in Kansas, for friends of slavery had moved into the state and

Abolitionist John Brown.

had drawn up a constitution that made slavery legal. In addition, two thousand abolitionists who refused to accept this constitution had moved in from the North. On election day, Missourians came over to vote and also led an attack on Lawrence, Kansas, the anti-slavery headquarters. In this attack, a dedicated abolitionist named John Brown called together a group of men and killed five pro-slavery settlers. Before the violent fighting was over, much property was destroyed and about two hundred persons were killed. The violence at Lawrence carried over into Congress itself, where senators attacked one another right on the floor of the Senate.

Then came the Dred Scott decision, a ruling of the United States Supreme Court. A slave named Dred Scott had been taken into a free territory and then back into Missouri. Scott sued in the courts for his freedom, but the courts ruled that he was not a citizen and that he had no right to sue. They said that although he had lived for a few years outside of a slave state, he was still not free. The Court also said that Congress had been wrong to ban slavery from the territories and that the Missouri Compromise was no longer in effect. Now, of course, slavery could be legal in any new territory where the settlers approved it. This was a great blow. It turned the cause of abolition into a national issue. Slavery became an issue that could break the nation into warring factions.

Southerners were very happy about the Dred Scott decision. They began to feel that they had won a victory, because the Supreme Court had said that when new settlers moved into the new territories they could take their property with them. And they considered their slaves to be their property. People in the North were more determined than ever before to prevent this from happening. In both the South and the North, those who opposed slavery and those who were for slavery began to close their ranks, just as an army does when it believes that a battle is coming.

Lawrence, Kansas, where violent fighting broke out over slavery.

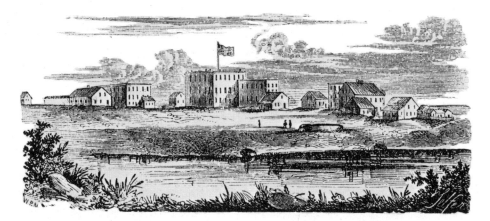

Dred Scott lost a Supreme Court battle to gain his freedom.

Then, something happened that no one could have anticipated. In 1859, the same John Brown who had led the rebellion in Kansas decided to seize the Federal armory at Harper's Ferry, Virginia.

United States Marines were sent out to capture John Brown and his men in Harper's Ferry, Virginia.

Brown gathered together some whites and some Negroes and marched on the armory. He hoped to capture arms and to free the slaves by force. A contingent of Marines was sent in. They put down the rebellion and captured Brown. The abolitionist leader was found guilty of treason and hanged.

The next year, 1860, Abraham Lincoln, a Republican, was elected President of the United States. It was well known both in the South and in the North that Lincoln was opposed to further extension of slavery in the territories. He had said, " 'A house divided against itself cannot stand.' " He had said, "I believe this government cannot endure permanently half slave and half free."

But, the house *was* divided, and nothing could stop the split from growing deeper. And, before Lincoln was sworn into office in March of 1861, seven slave states seceded — separated from — the Union. Four other states followed. April 21, 1861, was the fatal date in the history of our bloodiest war. This was the date when the South fired on the Federal forces who were holding Fort Sumter in South Carolina, and Lincoln realized, as did the rest of the nation, that the house divided against itself was beginning to fall apart. The Civil War, or the War Between the States, had begun.

What about the slaves? Did they know about the war, or its causes? Their masters had made sure that they could not read or write and did not talk about the war when their slaves were present. They did hear about the war, however, and they heard about "Father Lincoln," as they called him. They heard that this new President of the United States opposed slavery and that he would lead them out of bondage.

However, we must find out just what President Lincoln did think of slavery, before his election and after.

Lincoln hated slavery, but he was not an abolitionist. His early

68

In 1860, Abraham Lincoln, a Republican, was elected sixteenth President of the United States.

views had been that it would not have been right to free all the slaves without paying their owners for their losses. He had said that he did not believe that Congress had the right to interfere with the institution of slavery in the different states. Congress did have the power to abolish slavery in the District of Columbia, but only at the request of the people living there. Lincoln did believe that Congress should and could exclude slavery from the new lands of the West. The main reason was that he feared that the free labor of the slaves would make it hard for the new white settlers to make a living.

In addition, Lincoln had hoped that the slave owners would gradually free their slaves, if they were paid to do so. Abraham Lincoln was what we today would call a moderate. He was willing to compromise on the issue of slavery. This can be seen when, as President, he rejected the dividing of the new territories into free and slave states and insisted that slavery be forbidden in these new states. He did, however, promise to let slavery alone in the states where it already existed and to enforce the Fugitive Slave Law.

But, on the same day that Lincoln rejected the proposal to divide the territories into half free and half slave states, South Carolina seceded from the Union. The other southern states followed, and on February 8, 1861, the Confederate States of America was formed. Then, Confederate forces fired on Fort Sumter.

President Lincoln knew that he had to settle the most important question first. The question was whether in a free government the South had the right to break up the Union. The rebellion had to be put down. That was the most important job to be done.

President Lincoln went to war to preserve the Union. The leaders of the Confederacy and most white southerners went to war to preserve their right to have slaves. They were convinced that if they remained members of the Federal Union, they could not have this right. When they wrote their Confederate constitution, it contained this right — the right to have slaves — for themselves and for settlers of the new territories. The South based its right to secede and to fight against the North on this one issue — slavery.

President Lincoln and the northerners said that the Civil War was not based on slavery, but upon preserving the Union. It would have been fine, if the issue and the problems had been that simple. Soon, however, it had to be admitted that dealing with slavery and

Negroes building stockades for the Union Army.

the free Negroes was a problem that was right in the middle of the whole larger problem of the war itself. They could not be separated. The Civil War would have to settle both the right of states to secede from the Union and the slavery problem.

From the very beginning of the war, the Federal government did not know what to do with either the free blacks or slaves who had run away. Some fought at the side of Union soldiers, others at the side of the Confederates. Some were used as laborers in the camps in both armies. But, for the following reasons, none were permitted to enlist in the Union Army:

- Many white northerners feared that Negroes would demand political and social equality if they served in the Army.
- The Lincoln Administration had declared that this was not a war to end slavery but to preserve the Union, to end secession.
- Lincoln feared that if he permitted Negroes to enlist in the army, the slave owners in the border areas would not support the Union.
- Many northerners really believed that in spite of their good military record in former times, the Negroes just would not make good soldiers or sailors.

The war dragged on and the quick victory that the North expected did not come. The result was that late in 1862, President Lincoln finally permitted some Negroes to enlist in the armed forces.

The next action taken by President Lincoln was to offer to pay the slaveholders in the border states to free their slaves. Although

Drivers of a Union baggage train water their mules.

The 107th U.S. Colored Infantry.

this offer was not accepted, Lincoln did not order the slaves to be freed, because these territories would surely have gone over to the Confederates, if he had.

Slaves were freed in the District of Columbia, however, in 1862 by the payment of three hundred dollars for each slave. The people in the border states opposed this because they thought that soon they would lose their own slaves. The abolitionists were against it because they did not approve of the Federal government paying for something that no man had a right to own. Nobody was satisfied. The war went on.

It is hard to understand Lincoln's attitude on slavery, but perhaps this will explain it. Lincoln regarded secession as illegal. He therefore reasoned that the Confederate states were still in the Union. And, he had promised not to interfere with slavery in these states. The abolitionists criticized him for not acting swiftly to end slavery, and in the second year of the war, even those northerners who had not opposed slavery began to feel that it was the reason for the strength of the South: the southerners could go to war without worrying about their plantations because the slaves were there to carry on while they were fighting the war.

Negro riflemen during the Civil War.

Horace Greeley, editor of the New York *Tribune,* favored abolishing slavery and allowing unlimited numbers of Negroes to serve in the Union forces.

President Lincoln was widely criticized. One of the most prominent of his critics was Horace Greeley, editor of the New York *Tribune.* Greeley wanted Lincoln to abolish slavery and to permit the use of as many Negro troops as could be raised.

The President replied that his main object in the war was neither to save slavery nor destroy it. He said that if he could save the Union without freeing one slave he would do it, and if he could save it by freeing some of the slaves he would do that; that if he could save the Union by freeing some and leaving others alone, he would do that. He ended by saying that what he did about slavery and the colored race, he did because he believed it helped to save the Union.

But even before he had sent this answer to Greeley, Lincoln had really made up his mind that slavery would have to die if the nation were to live. He had already begun to compose the Emancipation

76

Negro families arriving in the Union lines.

Proclamation and had already read the first draft of it to his Cabinet.

The war had been going badly and Lincoln had finally come to realize that this would have to be a war against slavery as well as one to preserve the Union. On the advice of his Secretary of State, President Lincoln did not sign the preliminary Emancipation Proclamation until after the North had won a decisive victory at Antietam.

This first proclamation gave the southern states a chance to return to the Union, but the South rejected the offer.

The final Emancipation Proclamation was signed on January 1, 1863. It declared that all slaves in regions not under Federal control were free and urged that the newly freed slaves work faithfully for their wages, refrain from acts of violence against former masters, and enlist in the armed forces. It was not until after the Civil War was over and the Thirteenth Amendment was passed in 1865 that all slaves were actually freed.

The reason why all of the slaves were not freed by the Emancipation Proclamation is that it stated that all slaves in regions *not* under Federal control were to be free. Millions of slaves still lived in areas over which the North had no control, and another million lived in the border states. The proclamation was issued to raise the spirit of the Unionists and to win the support of foreign countries, especially England. These two objectives were realized.

What the Emancipation Proclamation did was to turn the war in favor of the North. It encouraged thousands of slaves to desert their owners and to join the Union Army. In the South, plantations could not be run without slaves and this meant that they were badly affected. And, the proclamation helped to unite antislavery groups in the North and in Europe. To the Negroes who were not freed, it gave new hope that soon their struggle would be over.

Many escaped slaves served in the Union Army.

Major Martin R. Delaney, one of the few Negro officers in the Union Army.

At this time, the great abolitionist Frederick Douglass began to recruit Negroes for the armed forces. Approximately 186,000 Negroes formed 166 Negro units. This was about 10 per cent of the Union forces. About three-fourths of these were former slaves. However, they were put into segrated units led by white officers and were not paid as much as the white soldiers or sailors. Only about a hundred Negroes were commissioned as officers and most of these were doctors and chaplains. Nevertheless, the Negroes fought with great honor and bravery and twenty-one Negroes won the Congressional Medal of Honor, the highest award the United States gives for courage and bravery on the field of battle. More than 38,000 Negroes lost their lives. Lincoln and his generals paid high tribute to the Negro soldiers and sailors on many occasions and regarded them as the most effective means to end the rebellion of the southern states. Negro soldiers helped the Union Army win several major battles in the last year and a half of the war. Not only did large numbers of Negroes fight in the Union Army, but between 200,000 and 300,000 Negroes served as laborers, spies, scouts, nurses, and medical attendants. When the war was over, the victory of the North over the South brought to an end the almost 250 years of slavery in the United States. It was called a Day of Jubilee, for now all men in the United States were free and their future seemed bright. In the Gettysburg Address, Lincoln had said, "This nation [was] conceived in liberty, and dedicated to the proposition that all men are created equal," and he had said that no nation could endure half slave and half free.

The southerners believed that the nation *could* endure half slave and half free. They did *not* believe that all men were created equal. The northerners believed just the opposite. And they were willing to go to war with others in their own country to prove that this

Negroes in Washington, D.C., celebrate the abolition of slavery.

nation could endure *only* if all men were free and equal. It took a bloody war and many years to determine which one was right. It *is* hard to believe, but it happened. Americans fought against one another and killed one another and believed that they were protecting themselves and their rights by doing so.

The Civil War ended in defeat for the South and in victory for the Union. But, it did not make the northerners happy, for they knew that they had fought against and killed their own people. The northerners did not feel that the war had ended in victory for the North, but had ended in peace, for all Americans. They felt that to make this a really free country and one united under laws that applied to all people in all of the states, the war had to be fought.

President Lincoln knew how much the southerners hated him. He knew how many had lost their lives in both the North and the South. He knew that there would be confusion and trouble as southerners tried to rebuild their lives. But he had confidence in all Americans. He looked to the future and not to the present for the solutions and the progress which he knew would come to both the South and to the North. He looked to the future when the Negroes would make the great contributions to the United States that they were capable of making. Today, we know that he was right.

Abraham Lincoln, the sixteenth President of the United States, did not live to see his dream realized. He lived only five days after General Lee's surrender at Appomattox, but he had seen the end of the Civil War, and he had asked that all Americans act ". . . with malice toward none; with charity toward all" to bind up the nation's wounds.

He must have known that the men of good faith in the Congress would pass, and that the required number of states would ratify, the Thirteenth Amendment. For so they did, by the end of the year

83

1865. And thus, slavery was forever outlawed in the United States. Now, at long last, the freed slaves believed what the Declaration of Independence had said — that all men *were* created equal and that all men *do have* the right to life, liberty, and the pursuit of happiness.

But the scars of slavery remain. The attitudes of white Americans toward black Americans have kept the descendants of slavery free in name only. Recent legislation is attempting to broaden the rights of all men. But, equal opportunities in housing, jobs, and education, and truly equal rights are for the most part still denied to Negro Americans. More than a hundred years after the Civil War, the black man is still seeking to secure his rights in America.

Suggestions For Further Reading

The American Negro: Old World Background and New World Experience. Rayford Logan and Irving Cohen. Houghton Mifflin.

The First Book of American Negroes. Margaret R. Young. Franklin Watts.

Flight to Freedom: The Story of the Underground Railroad. Henrietta Buckmaster. Thomas Y. Crowell.

Forever Free. The Story of the Emancipation Proclamation. Dorothy Sterling. Doubleday.

Four Took Freedom: Harriet Tubman, Frederick Douglass, Robert Smalls, and Blanche K. Bruce. Philip Sterling and Rayford Logan. Doubleday.

Frederick Douglass: Slave, Fighter, Freeman. Dorothy Sterling. Doubleday.

From Slavery to Freedom: A History of American Negroes. John Hope Franklin. Alfred A. Knopf.

Harriet Tubman: The Moses of Her People. Sarah Bradford. Corinth.

In Their Own Words: A History of the American Negro, vol. 1, 1619-1865. Thomas Y. Crowell.

Life and Times of Frederick Douglass. Frederick Douglass. Collier Books.

The Negro in America. Larry Cuban. Scott, Foresman.

Pioneers and Patriots: Six Negroes of the Colonial and Revolutionary Eras. Lavinia Dobler and Edgar A. Toppin. Doubleday.

There Once Was a Slave: The Heroic Story of Frederick Douglass. Shirley Graham. Messner.

Up From Slavery. Booker T. Washington. Doubleday.

Worth Fighting For: Negro During the Civil War and Reconstruction. Agnes McCarthy and Lawrence Reddick. Doubleday.

INDEX